ESSENTIAL ELEMENTS®

GUITAR ENSEMBLES

CHRISTMAS SONGS

T0081857

ISBN-13: 978-1-4234-3159-6
ISBN-10: 1-4234-3159-6

HAL•LEONARD®
CORPORATION

7777 W. BLUEMOUND RD. P.O. BOX 13819 MILWAUKEE, WI 53213

Visit Hal Leonard Online at
www.halleonard.com

CONTENTS

BLUE CHRISTMAS

Words and Music by Billy Hayes and Jay Johnson

DO YOU HEAR WHAT I HEAR

Words and Music by Noel Regney and Gloria Shayne

THE CHRISTMAS SONG
(Chestnuts Roasting on an Open Fire)

Music and Lyric by Mel Torme and Robert Wells

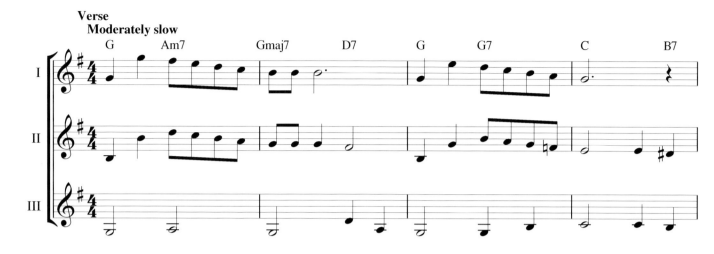

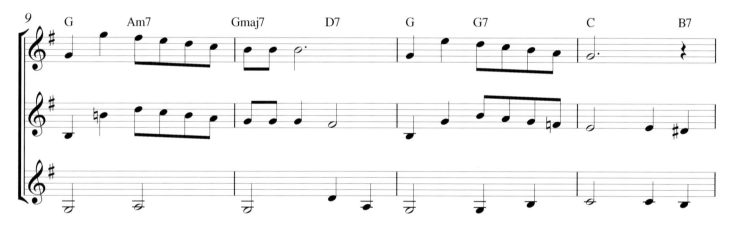

Bridge

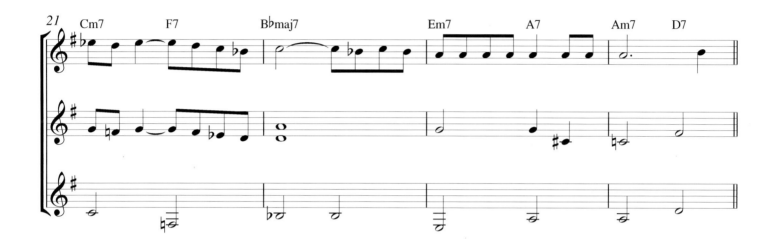

Outro-Verse

CHRISTMAS TIME IS HERE

from A CHARLIE BROWN CHRISTMAS

Words by Lee Mendelson
Music by Vince Guaraldi

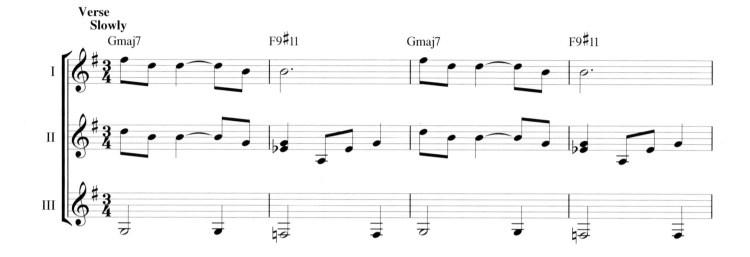

FROSTY THE SNOW MAN

Words and Music by Steve Nelson and Jack Rollins

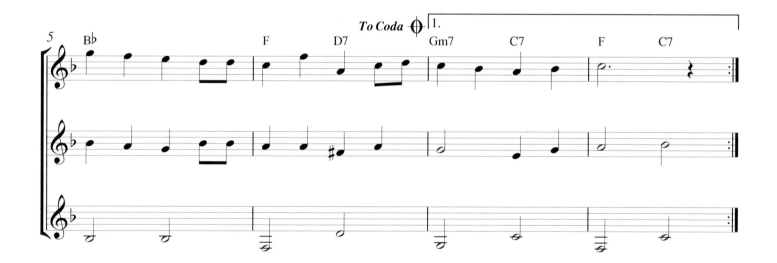

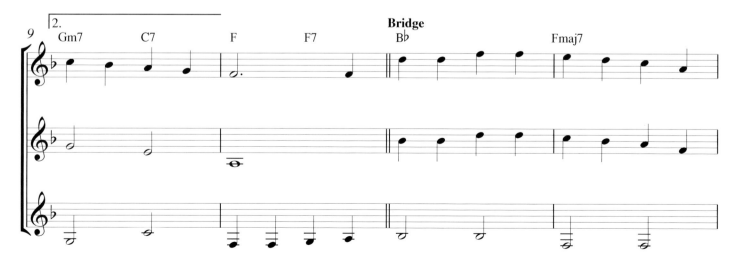

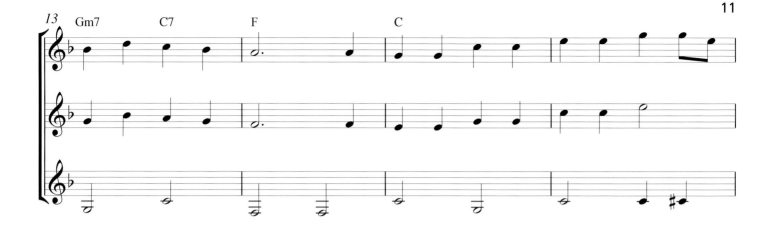

Coda

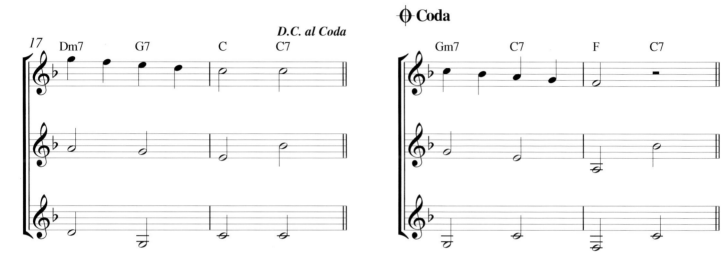

HERE COMES SANTA CLAUS
(Right Down Santa Claus Lane)

Words and Music by Gene Autry and Oakley Haldeman

LET IT SNOW! LET IT SNOW! LET IT SNOW!

Words by Sammy Cahn
Music by Jule Styne

A HOLLY JOLLY CHRISTMAS

Music and Lyrics by Johnny Marks

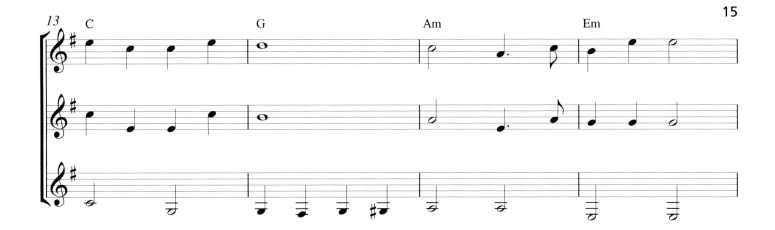

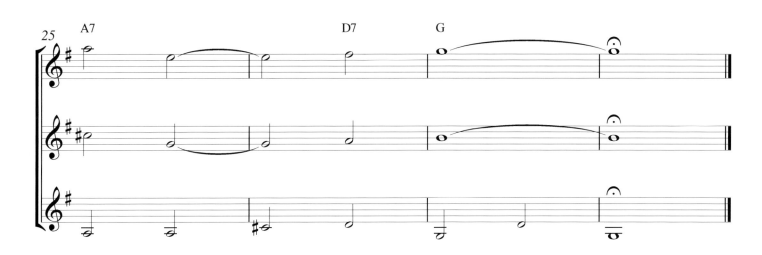

I'LL BE HOME FOR CHRISTMAS

Words and Music by Kim Gannon and Walter Kent

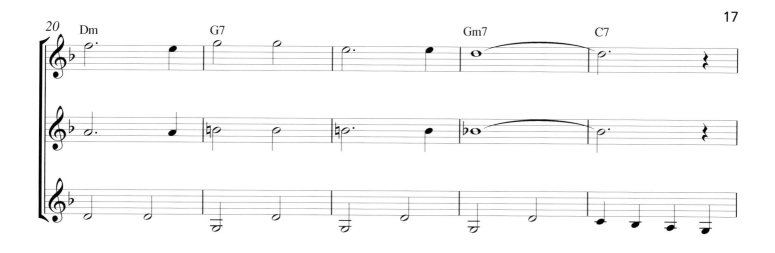

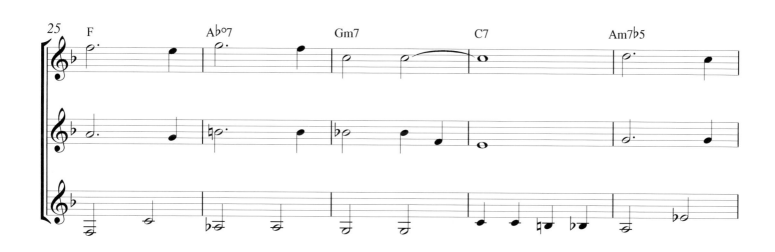

JINGLE-BELL ROCK

Words and Music by Joe Beal and Jim Boothe

Outro-Verse

To Coda ⊕

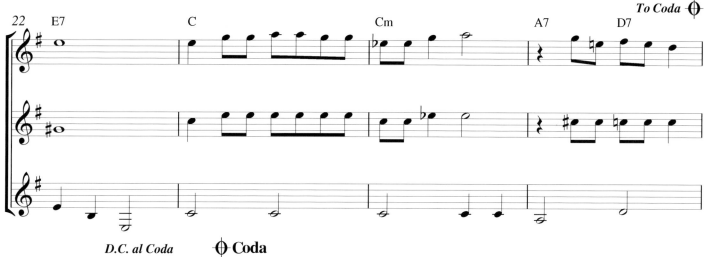

D.C. al Coda
(take repeat)

⊕ **Coda**

MY FAVORITE THINGS

from THE SOUND OF MUSIC

Lyrics by Oscar Hammerstein II
Music by Richard Rodgers

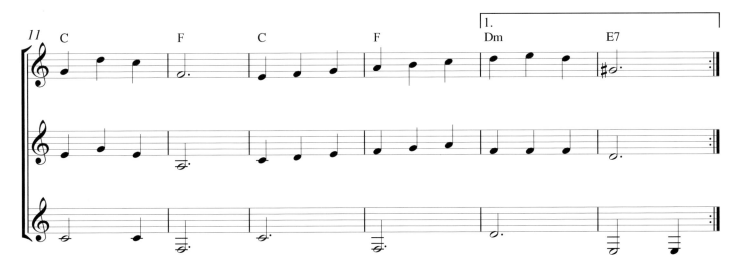

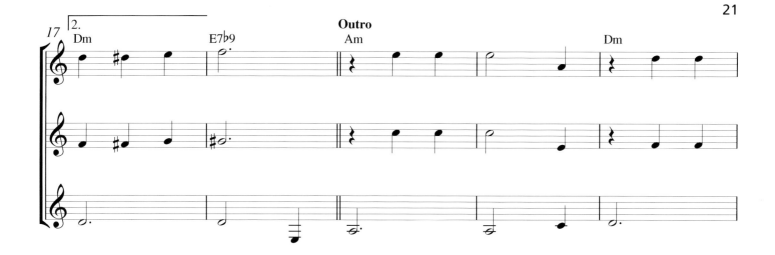

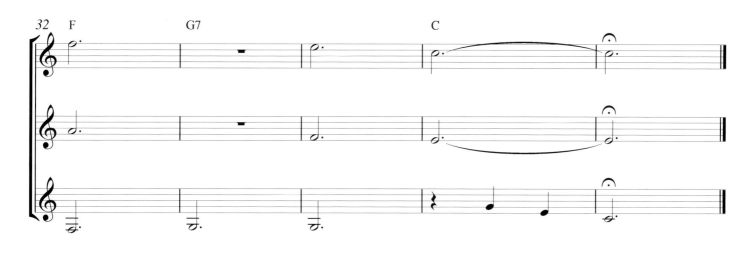

ROCKIN' AROUND THE CHRISTMAS TREE

Music and Lyrics by Johnny Marks

Outro-Verse

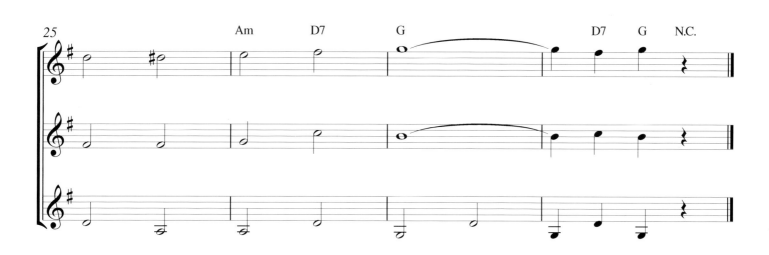

RUDOLPH THE RED-NOSED REINDEER

Music and Lyrics by Johnny Marks

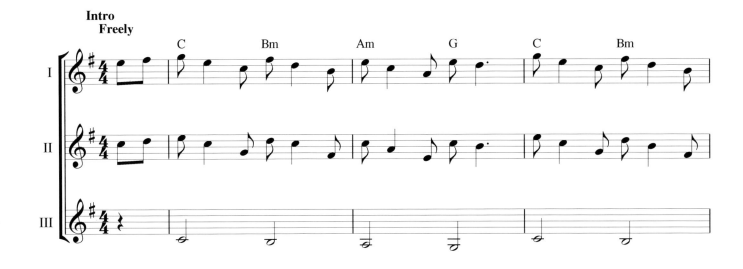

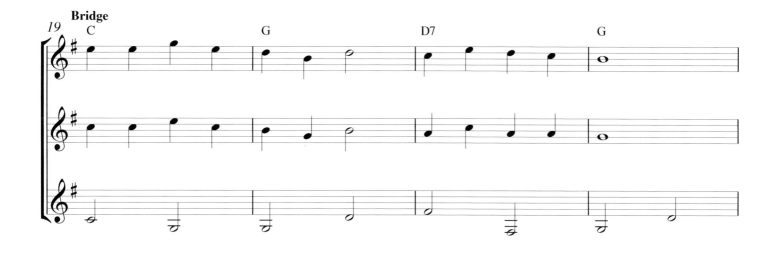

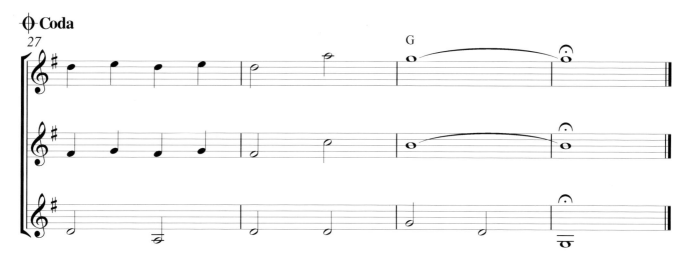

SANTA CLAUS IS COMIN' TO TOWN

Words by Haven Gillespie
Music by J. Fred Coots

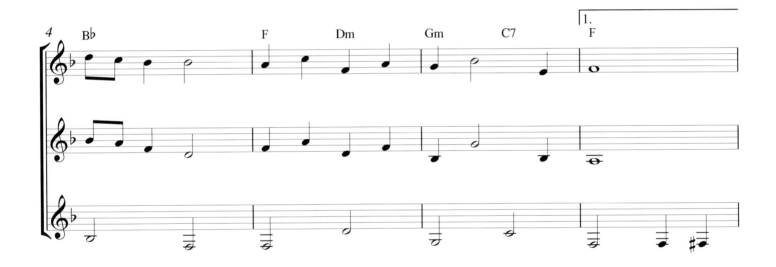

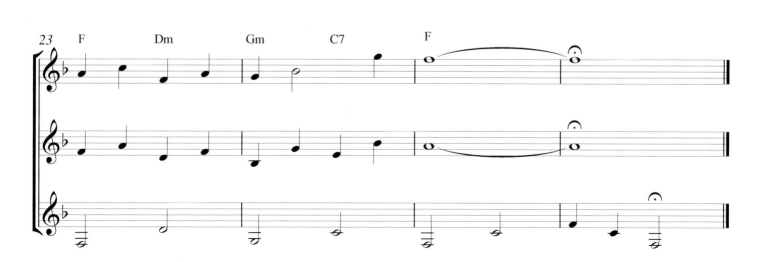

SILVER BELLS

from the Paramount Picture THE LEMON DROP KID

Words and Music by Jay Livingston and Ray Evans

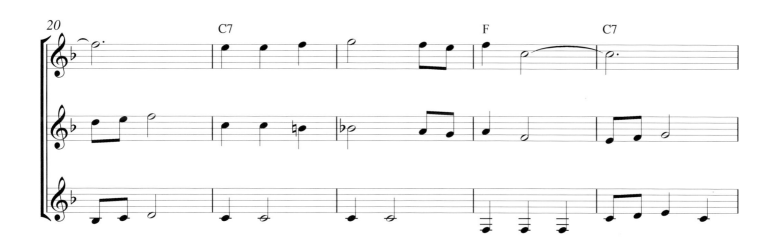

Hal•Leonard GUITAR PLAY-ALONG

Complete song lists available online.

This series will help you play your favorite songs quickly and easily. Just follow **INCLUDES TAB** the tab and listen to the audio to the hear how the guitar should sound, and then play along using the separate backing tracks. Audio files also include software to slow down the tempo without changing pitch. The melody and lyrics are included in the book so that you can sing or simply follow along.

HAL•LEONARD®
www.halleonard.com

EASY GUITAR
WITH NOTES & TAB

This series features simplified arrangements with notes, tab, chord charts, and strum and pick patterns.

MIXED FOLIOS

00702287	Acoustic	$19.99
00702002	Acoustic Rock Hits for Easy Guitar	$17.99
00702166	All-Time Best Guitar Collection	$29.99
00702232	Best Acoustic Songs for Easy Guitar	$16.99
00119835	Best Children's Songs	$16.99
00703055	The Big Book of Nursery Rhymes & Children's Songs	$16.99
00698978	Big Christmas Collection	$19.99
00702394	Bluegrass Songs for Easy Guitar	$15.99
00289632	Bohemian Rhapsody	$19.99
00703387	Celtic Classics	$16.99
00224808	Chart Hits of 2016-2017	$14.99
00267383	Chart Hits of 2017-2018	$14.99
00334293	Chart Hits of 2019-2020	$16.99
00403479	Chart Hits of 2021-2022	$16.99
00702149	Children's Christian Songbook	$9.99
00702028	Christmas Classics	$9.99
00101779	Christmas Guitar	$16.99
00702141	Classic Rock	$8.95
00159642	Classical Melodies	$12.99
00253933	Disney/Pixar's Coco	$19.99
00702203	CMT's 100 Greatest Country Songs	$34.99
00702283	The Contemporary Christian Collection	$16.99
00196954	Contemporary Disney	$19.99
00702239	Country Classics for Easy Guitar	$24.99
00702257	Easy Acoustic Guitar Songs	$17.99
00702041	Favorite Hymns for Easy Guitar	$12.99
00222701	Folk Pop Songs	$19.99
00126894	Frozen	$14.99
00333922	Frozen 2	$14.99
00702286	Glee	$16.99
00702160	The Great American Country Songbook	$19.99
00702148	Great American Gospel for Guitar	$14.99
00702050	Great Classical Themes for Easy Guitar	$9.99
00148030	Halloween Guitar Songs	$17.99
00702273	Irish Songs	$14.99
00192503	Jazz Classics for Easy Guitar	$16.99
00702275	Jazz Favorites for Easy Guitar	$17.99
00702274	Jazz Standards for Easy Guitar	$19.99
00702162	Jumbo Easy Guitar Songbook	$24.99
00232285	La La Land	$16.99
00702258	Legends of Rock	$14.99
00702189	MTV's 100 Greatest Pop Songs	$34.99
00702272	1950s Rock	$16.99
00702271	1960s Rock	$16.99
00702270	1970s Rock	$24.99
00702269	1980s Rock	$16.99
00702268	1990s Rock	$24.99
00369043	Rock Songs for Kids	$14.99
00109725	Once	$14.99
00702187	Selections from O Brother Where Art Thou?	$19.99
00702178	100 Songs for Kids	$16.99
00702515	Pirates of the Caribbean	$17.99
00702125	Praise and Worship for Guitar	$14.99
00287930	Songs from *A Star Is Born, The Greatest Showman, La La Land,* and More Movie Musicals	$16.99
00702285	Southern Rock Hits	$12.99
00156420	Star Wars Music	$16.99
00121535	30 Easy Celtic Guitar Solos	$16.99
00244654	Top Hits of 2017	$14.99
00283786	Top Hits of 2018	$14.99
00302269	Top Hits of 2019	$14.99
00355779	Top Hits of 2020	$14.99
00374083	Top Hits of 2021	$16.99
00702294	Top Worship Hits	$17.99
00702255	VH1's 100 Greatest Hard Rock Songs	$39.99
00702175	VH1's 100 Greatest Songs of Rock and Roll	$34.99
00702253	Wicked	$12.99

ARTIST COLLECTIONS

00702267	AC/DC for Easy Guitar	$17.99
00156221	Adele – 25	$16.99
00396889	Adele – 30	$19.99
00702040	Best of the Allman Brothers	$16.99
00702865	J.S. Bach for Easy Guitar	$15.99
00702169	Best of The Beach Boys	$16.99
00702292	The Beatles — 1	$22.99
00125796	Best of Chuck Berry	$16.99
00702201	The Essential Black Sabbath	$15.99
00702250	blink-182 — Greatest Hits	$19.99
02501615	Zac Brown Band — The Foundation	$19.99
02501621	Zac Brown Band — You Get What You Give	$16.99
00702043	Best of Johnny Cash	$19.99
00702090	Eric Clapton's Best	$16.99
00702086	Eric Clapton — from the Album Unplugged	$17.99
00702202	The Essential Eric Clapton	$19.99
00702053	Best of Patsy Cline	$17.99
00222697	Very Best of Coldplay – 2nd Edition	$17.99
00702229	The Very Best of Creedence Clearwater Revival	$16.99
00702145	Best of Jim Croce	$16.99
00702278	Crosby, Stills & Nash	$12.99
14042809	Bob Dylan	$15.99
00702276	Fleetwood Mac — Easy Guitar Collection	$17.99
00139462	The Very Best of Grateful Dead	$17.99
00702136	Best of Merle Haggard	$19.99
00702227	Jimi Hendrix — Smash Hits	$19.99
00702288	Best of Hillsong United	$12.99
00702236	Best of Antonio Carlos Jobim	$15.99
00702245	Elton John — Greatest Hits 1970–2002	$19.99
00129855	Jack Johnson	$17.99
00702204	Robert Johnson	$16.99
00702234	Selections from Toby Keith — 35 Biggest Hits	$12.95
00702003	Kiss	$16.99
00702216	Lynyrd Skynyrd	$17.99
00702182	The Essential Bob Marley	$17.99
00146081	Maroon 5	$14.99
00121925	Bruno Mars – Unorthodox Jukebox	$12.99
00702248	Paul McCartney — All the Best	$14.99
00125484	The Best of MercyMe	$12.99
00702209	Steve Miller Band — Young Hearts (Greatest Hits)	$12.95
00124167	Jason Mraz	$15.99
00702096	Best of Nirvana	$17.99
00702211	The Offspring — Greatest Hits	$17.99
00138026	One Direction	$17.99
00702030	Best of Roy Orbison	$17.99
00702144	Best of Ozzy Osbourne	$14.99
00702279	Tom Petty	$17.99
00102911	Pink Floyd	$17.99
00702139	Elvis Country Favorites	$19.99
00702293	The Very Best of Prince	$22.99
00699415	Best of Queen for Guitar	$16.99
00109279	Best of R.E.M.	$14.99
00702208	Red Hot Chili Peppers — Greatest Hits	$19.99
00198960	The Rolling Stones	$17.99
00174793	The Very Best of Santana	$16.99
00702196	Best of Bob Seger	$16.99
00146046	Ed Sheeran	$19.99
00702252	Frank Sinatra — Nothing But the Best	$12.99
00702010	Best of Rod Stewart	$17.99
00702049	Best of George Strait	$17.99
00702259	Taylor Swift for Easy Guitar	$15.99
00359800	Taylor Swift – Easy Guitar Anthology	$24.99
00702260	Taylor Swift — Fearless	$14.99
00139727	Taylor Swift — 1989	$19.99
00115960	Taylor Swift — Red	$16.99
00253667	Taylor Swift — Reputation	$17.99
00702290	Taylor Swift — Speak Now	$16.99
00232849	Chris Tomlin Collection – 2nd Edition	$14.99
00702226	Chris Tomlin — See the Morning	$12.95
00148643	Train	$14.99
00702427	U2 — 18 Singles	$19.99
00702108	Best of Stevie Ray Vaughan	$17.99
00279005	The Who	$14.99
00702123	Best of Hank Williams	$15.99
00194548	Best of John Williams	$14.99
00702228	Neil Young — Greatest Hits	$17.99
00119133	Neil Young — Harvest	$16.99

Prices, contents and availability subject to change without notice.

Visit Hal Leonard online at halleonard.com

Celebrate Christmas

WITH YOUR GUITAR AND HAL LEONARD

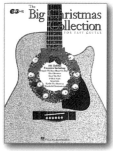
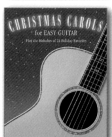

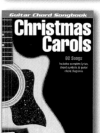

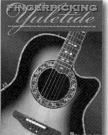

THE BEST CHRISTMAS GUITAR FAKE BOOK EVER

Over 150 Christmas classics for guitar. Songs include: Blue Christmas • The Chipmunk Song • Frosty the Snow Man • Happy Holiday • A Holly Jolly Christmas • I Saw Mommy Kissing Santa Claus • I Wonder As I Wander • Jingle-Bell Rock • Rudolph, the Red-Nosed Reindeer • Santa Bring My Baby Back (To Me) • Suzy Snowflake • Tennessee Christmas • and more.

00240053 Melody/Lyrics/Chords $29.99

THE BIG CHRISTMAS COLLECTION FOR EASY GUITAR

Includes over 70 Christmas favorites, such as: Ave Maria • Blue Christmas • Deck the Hall • Feliz Navidad • Frosty the Snow Man • Happy Holiday • A Holly Jolly Christmas • Joy to the World • O Holy Night • Silver and Gold • Suzy Snowflake • and more. Does not include TAB.

00698978 Easy Guitar $19.99

CHRISTMAS CAROLS
For Easy Guitar

24 holiday favorites, including: Carol of the Bells • Good King Wenceslas • Hark! the Herald Angels Sing • I Saw Three Ships • Jingle Bells • Jolly Old St. Nicholas • O Come, O Come Immanuel • O Little Town of Bethlehem • Up on the Housetop • and more. Does not include TAB.

00702221 Easy Guitar $10.99

CHRISTMAS CAROLS
Guitar Chord Songbook

80 favorite carols for guitarists who just need the lyrics and chords: Angels We Have Heard on High • Away in a Manger • Deck the Hall • Good King Wenceslas • The Holly and the Ivy • Irish Carol • Jingle Bells • Joy to the World • O Holy Night • Rocking • Silent Night • Up on the Housetop • Welsh Carol • What Child Is This? • and more.

00699536 Lyrics/Chord Symbols/
              Guitar Chord Diagrams $14.99

CLASSICAL GUITAR CHRISTMAS SHEET MUSIC

30 top holiday songs: Away in a Manger • Deck the Hall • Go, Tell It on the Mountain • Hallelujah Chorus • I Saw Three Ships • Jingle Bells • O Little Town of Bethlehem • Silent Night • The Twelve Days of Christmas • Up on the Housetop • We Wish You a Merry Christmas • What Child Is This? • and more. Does not include TAB.

00146974 Solo Classical Guitar $10.99

CHRISTMAS JAZZ
Jazz Guitar Chord Melody Solos

21 songs in chord-melody style for the beginning to intermediate jazz guitarist in standard notation and tablature: Auld Lang Syne • Baby, It's Cold Outside • Cool Yule • Have Yourself a Merry Little Christmas • Mary, Did You Know? • Santa Baby • White Christmas • Winter Wonderland • and more.

00171334 Solo Guitar..........................$15.99

CHRISTMAS SONGS FOR EASY GUITAR

20 classic Christmas tunes: Blue Christmas • The Christmas Song (Chestnuts Roasting) • Frosty the Snow Man • Christmas Time Is Here • A Holly Jolly Christmas • I Saw Mommy Kissing Santa Claus • I'll Be Home for Christmas • Jingle-Bell Rock • Merry Christmas, Darling • Rudolph the Red-Nosed Reindeer • Silver Bells • You're All I Want for Christmas • and more.

00699804 Easy Guitar $9.99

FINGERPICKING CHRISTMAS SONGS

15 songs for intermediate-level guitarists, combining melody and harmony in superb fingerpicking arrangements: Baby, It's Cold Outside • Caroling, Caroling • Have Yourself a Merry Little Christmas • I Heard the Bells on Christmas Day • The Little Drummer Boy • Mary, Did You Know? • Mele Kalikimaka • Sleigh Ride • White Christmas • Wonderful Christmastime • and more.

00171333 Fingerstyle Guitar $10.99

FINGERPICKING YULETIDE

Carefully written for intermediate-level guitarists, this collection includes an introduction to fingerstyle guitar and 16 holiday favorites: Do You Hear What I Hear • Happy Xmas (War Is Over) • A Holly Jolly Christmas • Jingle-Bell Rock • Rudolph the Red-Nosed Reindeer • and more.

00699654 Fingerstyle Guitar $12.99

FIRST 50 CHRISTMAS CAROLS YOU SHOULD PLAY ON GUITAR

Accessible, must-know Christmas songs are included in this collection arranged for guitar solo with a combo of tab, chords and lyrics. Includes: Angels We Have Heard on High • The First Noel • God Rest Ye Merry, Gentlemen • The Holly and the Ivy • O Christmas Tree • Silent Night • Up on the Housetop • What Child Is This? • and more.

00236224 Guitar Solo..........................$12.99

3-CHORD CHRISTMAS

You only need to know how to play 3 chords (G, C and D) on guitar to master these 25 holiday favorites: Away in a Manger • The Chipmunk Song • Frosty the Snow Man • Go, Tell It on the Mountain • Here Comes Santa Claus • Jingle Bells • The Little Drummer Boy • O Christmas Tree • Silent Night • Silver Bells • While Shepherds Watched Their Flocks • and more.

00146973 Guitar Solo..........................$10.99

THE ULTIMATE GUITAR CHRISTMAS FAKE BOOK

200 Christmas standards: All I Want for Christmas Is You • Baby, It's Cold Outside • The Christmas Song (Chestnuts Roasting on an Open Fire) • Do You Want to Build a Snowman? • Feliz Navidad • Frosty the Snow Man • A Holly Jolly Christmas • Jingle Bells • Let It Snow! Let It Snow! Let It Snow! • Mary, Did You Know? • Rockin' Around the Christmas Tree • Santa Baby • Silent Night • What Child Is This? • White Christmas • and more.

00236446 Melody/Lyrics/Chords $29.99

HAL•LEONARD®

www.halleonard.com

Prices, contents and availability subject to change without notice.